NOTE: EVEN IF YOUR PARENTS
DON'T LOOK **ANYTHING AT ALL**
LIKE THIS...

THIS BOOK IS STILL **FOR YOU**, BECAUSE
EVERY PARENT IN THE WORLD HAS STUFF IN COMMON

QUICKLY TURN OVER  THING IS!

HOT NEWS!

YEP, THAT'S RIGHT,
TO CREATE YOU, YOUR
PARENTS MADE LOVE (LIKE
BILLIONS OF PARENTS ALL
OVER THE WORLD)

THEY DIDN'T BUY
YOU AT THE
SUPERMARKET

THEY DIDN'T FIND
YOU UNDER A
GOOSEBERRY BUSH

AND AS FOR THE STORK BRINGING YOU—
THAT'S JUST **TOTAL GARBAGE!**

WARNING!

THE AUTHOR OF THIS BOOK HAS **22** CHILDREN
(INCLUDING **3** SETS OF TWINS AND **3** SETS OF TRIPLETS),
SO SHE KNOWS WHAT SHE'S TALKING ABOUT!

JUST TAKE A LOOK AT HER BATHROOM...

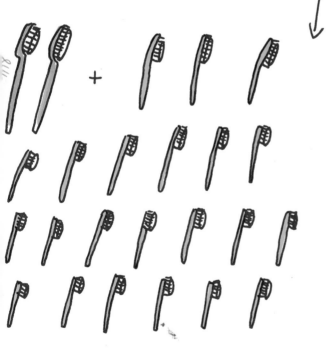

FAMILY-SIZE STRAWBERRY GUMDROP FLAVORED TOOTHPASTE

5 LBS.

WORDS AND DRAWINGS BY FRANÇOIZE BOUCHER
(HELPED BY LOU BOUCHER)

WALKER BOOKS FOR YOUNG READERS
AN IMPRINT OF BLOOMSBURY
NEW YORK   LONDON   NEW DELHI   SYDNEY

INTRODUCTION
So just how did you get your parents?

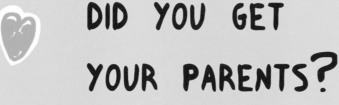

HEL-*LOOOO*, SUPEREGG HERE!
IF IT WASN'T FOR ME,
YOU WOULDN'T EXIST!

GREAT BIG SHOW-OFF

AND................

THE OFFICIAL DEFINITION OF "PARENTS"

2 HUMAN BEINGS (OFTEN WEIRD) WHOSE HOME YOU LAND IN **WITHOUT HAVING ASKED TO,** WHO LOVE YOU MORE THAN ANYTHING ELSE IN THE WORLD AND...WHO CAN SOMETIMES BE **A BIG PAIN**

THE DICTIONARY THAT TELLS THE TRUTH, **THE WHOLE TRUTH, AND NOTHING BUT THE TRUTH...**

YOU MIGHT
THINK THAT YOUR
MOM AND DAD
ARE (ALMOST)
ORDINARY
HUMAN BEINGS

THEY LOOK AND DRESS JUST LIKE EVERYBODY ELSE (AND OFTEN MAKE STUPID COMMENTS)

BUT IN FACT THEY ARE AMAZING CREATURES

THEY'VE GOT <u>HUGE</u> MAGIC HEARTS THAT LOVE YOU 24/7 (EVEN WHEN YOU'RE TOTALLY UNBEARABLE)

PROOF (COMPARE THE SIZES)

PARENT'S HEART

I REALLY WANT A CHEESEBURGER

MEGA-FAT MAMMOTH

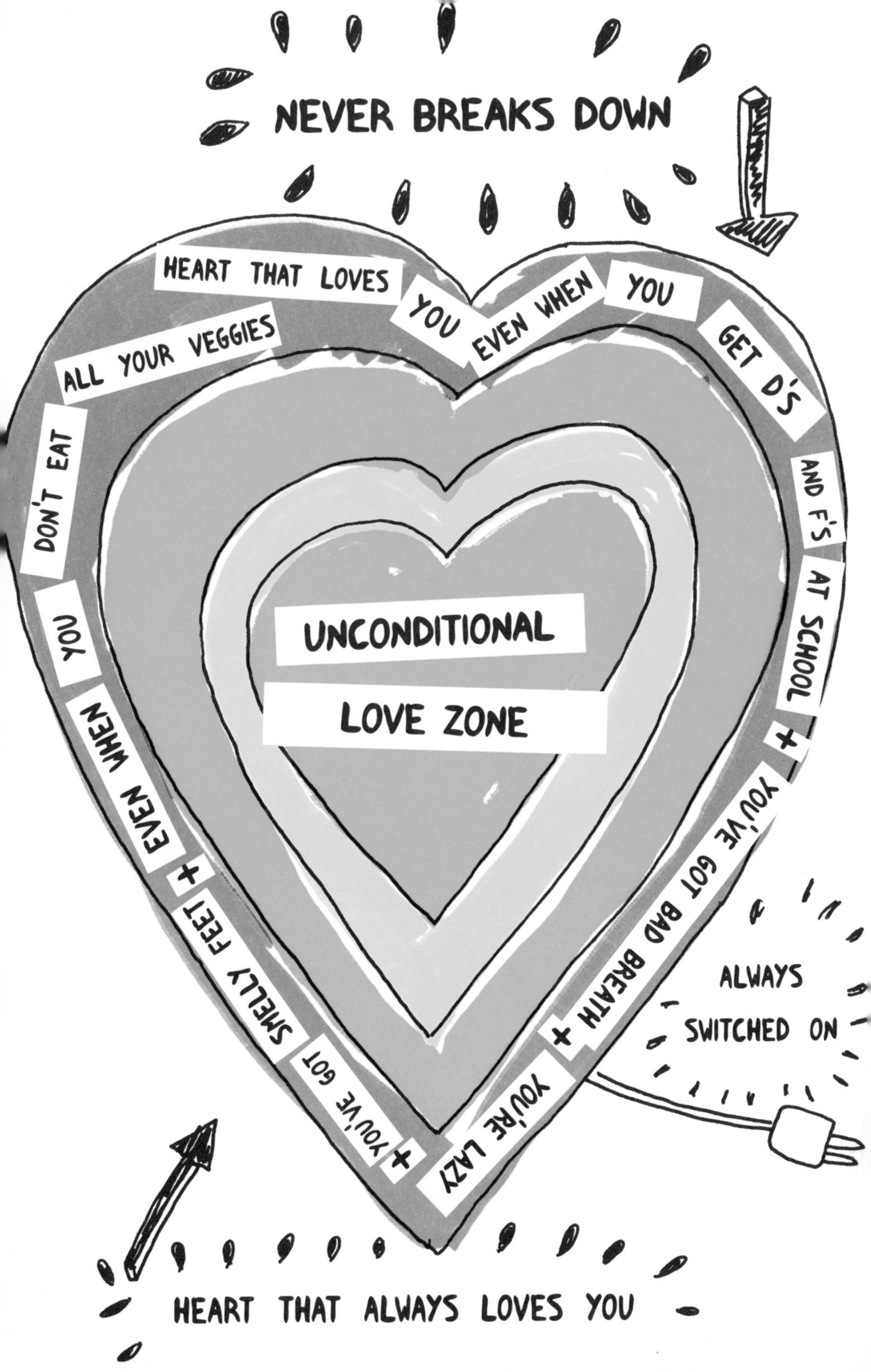
NEVER BREAKS DOWN
HEART THAT LOVES
YOU
EVEN WHEN
YOU
GET D'S
AND F'S
AT SCHOOL
+
YOU'VE GOT BAD BREATH
+
YOU'RE LAZY
+
YOU'VE GOT
SMELLY FEET
+
EVEN WHEN
YOU
DON'T EAT
ALL YOUR VEGGIES
UNCONDITIONAL
LOVE ZONE
ALWAYS
SWITCHED ON
HEART THAT ALWAYS LOVES YOU

If someone upsets you, your parents can <u>CHANGE.</u> They become fiercely protective in one second flat

INCREDIBLE!

<u>EXAMPLE:</u> WATCH WHAT HAPPENS IF SOMEONE CALLS YOU A **BIG PEA-BRAINED IDIOT** IN FRONT OF THEM

GRRRRR

SEEING RED

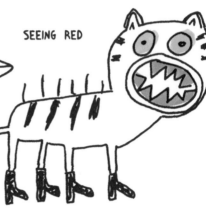

YOUR MOM

ANGRY TIGRESS

ROAAAR

YOUR DAD

FEROCIOUS LION

But **WATCH OUT** BECAUSE THIS CAN WORK BOTH WAYS. IF YOU GO TOO FAR, THEY CAN TURN INTO SCARY **FIRE-BREATHING** DRAGONS

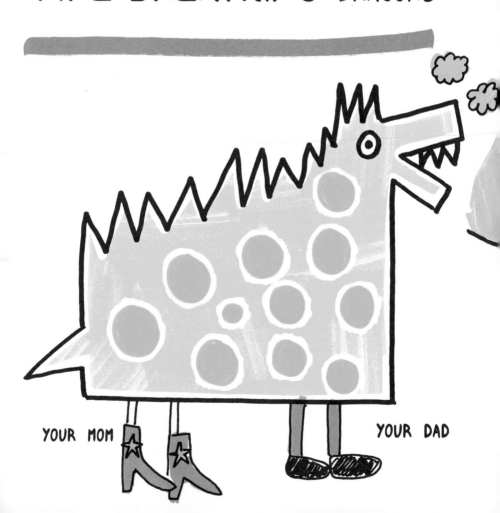

YOUR MOM   YOUR DAD

YOUR PARENTS ARE
SUPER SMART
AT SOLVING YOUR PROBLEMS, SO **ALWAYS** TELL THEM IF YOU HAVE ANY

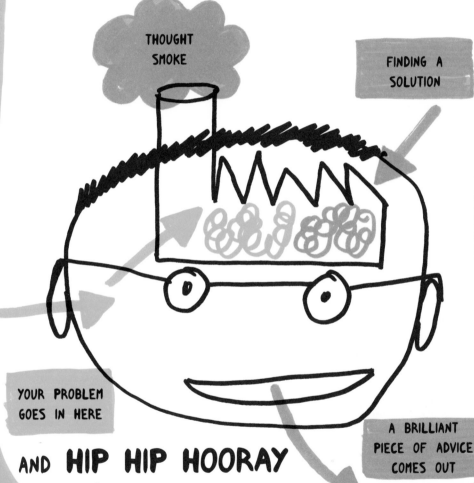

THEY HAVE PROBLEM-SOLVING FACTORIES INSIDE THEIR HEADS.

THOUGHT SMOKE

FINDING A SOLUTION

YOUR PROBLEM GOES IN HERE

AND **HIP HIP HOORAY** IT'S ALL FIXED!

A BRILLIANT PIECE OF ADVICE COMES OUT

PHEW!

YOUR MOM AND DAD ARE YOUR ANCESTORS. THEY'VE BEEN ON THIS EARTH A LOT LONGER THAN YOU HAVE, SO THEY'VE GOT <u>**TONS OF LIFE EXPERIENCE**</u>...

DINO, YOUR DAD'S FRIEND
(THEY WERE AT SCHOOL TOGETHER AGES AGO)

STEGOSOMETHINGSAURUS

YOU KNOW, YOUR DAD FAILED HIS EXAMS 3 TIMES, HE JUST NEVER TOLD YOU

...AND CAN GIVE YOU LOADS OF MEGA INTELLIGENT ADVICE

MR. AND MRS. STONE AGE (BORN BEFORE THE INVENTION OF THE INTERNET, FACEBOOK, HIGH-SPEED TRAINS, COCOA PUFFS, AND CELL PHONES)

You've got to agree that your parents are TOTAL MAGICIANS

1. IT STARTS WHEN YOU'RE BORN (THEY CAN'T GET OVER IT)

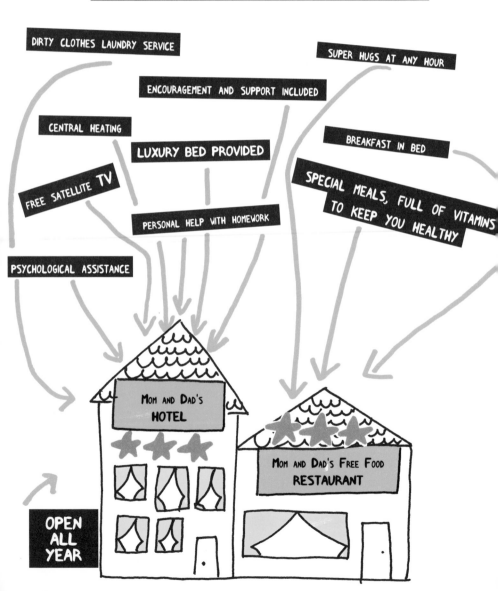

But <u>ALL THE SAME</u>
DON'T ASK FOR TOO MUCH

YOU MUST BE JOKING!

FREEZE! I NEED $250,000 RIGHT THIS MINUTE TO PUT A MOVIE THEATER IN MY BEDROOM

YOUR SKI HAT WITH EYE HOLES

<u>YOU IN DISGUISE</u>

HOSE FOR EXTRA PERSUASION POWER

YOUR MOM AND DAD ARE GENEROUS
BUT THEY AREN'T MILLIONAIRES

NOTE: IF BY ANY CHANCE THEY ARE, PLEASE
SEND THEIR BANK DETAILS **IMMEDIATELY**
TO THE AUTHOR OF THIS BOOK

Even though it's sometimes very difficult, your parents do everything they can to **BRING YOU UP RIGHT**

But why is being brought up right important? Just look at the diagram ⟶

AND FINALLY, HERE'S THE PROOF THAT YOUR PARENTS **LOVE YOU MORE THAN ANYTHING ELSE IN THE WORLD**

(EVEN WHEN YOU INFURIATE THEM)

HERE'S ANOTHER REALLY AWESOME THING ABOUT PARENTS

EVERY DAY THEY DO **EVERYTHING** THEY CAN TO MAKE YOU **AS HAPPY AS POSSIBLE**

COMPARED TO THEM, SANTA CLAUS IS A TOTAL RIP-OFF AS HE ONLY COMES ONCE A YEAR

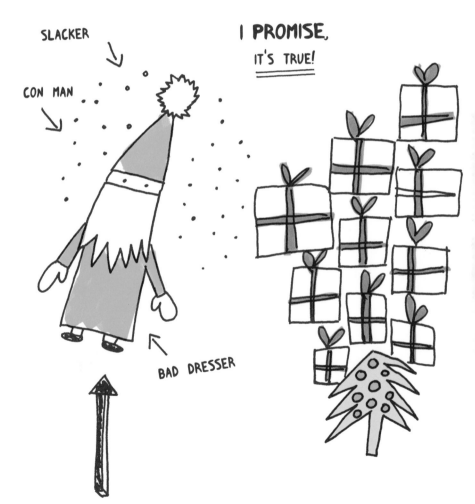

BIG FAT COUCH POTATO

BUT

In spite of all their super-good points, your parents do still annoy you a lot

Don't worry, it's
NORMAL

IT'S THE
SAME IN
EVERY
FAMILY

THE BAD NEWS IS...

SUPER-PERFECT PARENTS
DON'T EXIST !!!

(SUPER-PERFECT CHILDREN DON'T EXIST EITHER)

SHOCK! HORROR!

ALWAYS CALM AND SMILING

ALWAYS UNDERSTAND YOU 100%

NEVER SHOUT AT YOU FOR NO REASON

BUY A CONSTANT SUPPLY OF CANDY

HAVE DECIDED TO LIVE AT DISNEY WORLD ALL YEAR ROUND

NEVER MAKE YOU DO CHORES

MR. AND MRS. BESTPARENTSEVER

 THE GOOD NEWS IS...

SO WHAT! IT'S MUCH MORE FUN TO HAVE PARENTS WITH FAULTS!

HERE'S SOMETHING VERY ANNOYING: YOUR PARENTS ALWAYS TELL YOU TO HURRY UP

>⧸ OPTION 1 ⧹>

GIVE THEM A DOSE OF **CALMDOWN-DEAR** MEDICINE

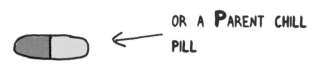

OR A **PARENT** CHILL PILL

CAN YOU STOP BOTHERING ME!

WHERE'S THE FIRE?

IS THE WORLD ENDING?

IS THERE A TRAIN TO CATCH?

A ROCKET IN YOUR POCKET?

I ♥ BEING LAZY

RING
RING
RING

WHY ARE
ALL PARENTS
OBSESSED WITH
GOOD MANNERS?

IT'S SIMPLE,
THEY DON'T WANT YOU TO
HAVE THE SAME HORRIBLE
EXPERIENCE AS THIS GUY

THE FAMOUS ISTAAC MYFINGERUPMYNOSE, AGED 102

(HE STUCK HIS FINGER UP HIS NOSE WHEN HE WAS 5 AND IT'S BEEN THERE EVER SINCE)

HIS SPECIAL CAR

HIS HAT

OH DARN!

AND, COMING SOON, HIS SPECIALLY MADE COFFIN

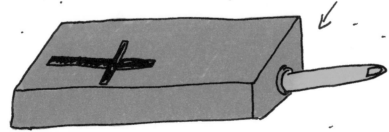

A RIDDLE

WHAT'S THE DIFFERENCE BETWEEN AN OVEN FROM THE FUTURE AND YOU?

CLEANLINESS NEWS FLASH

THAT'S WHY YOUR PARENTS ARE ALWAYS ON YOU TO TAKE A BATH AND **RIGHTLY SO**

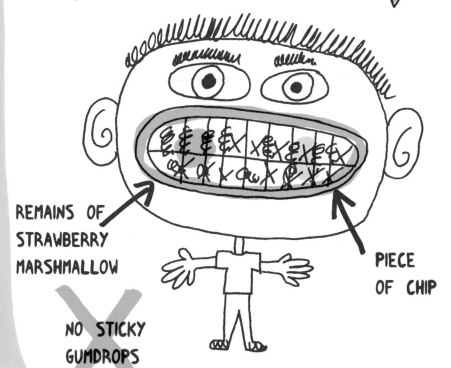

BUT IN 2032, YOU'LL THANK THEM FOR IT!

WHEN YOU'RE A HOLLYWOOD STAR

YOU, IN

THE MAN WITH THE BIONIC SMILE

OR THE MULTI-BILLIONAIRE STAR OF TOOTHPASTE ADS

COLGATE®

BLING

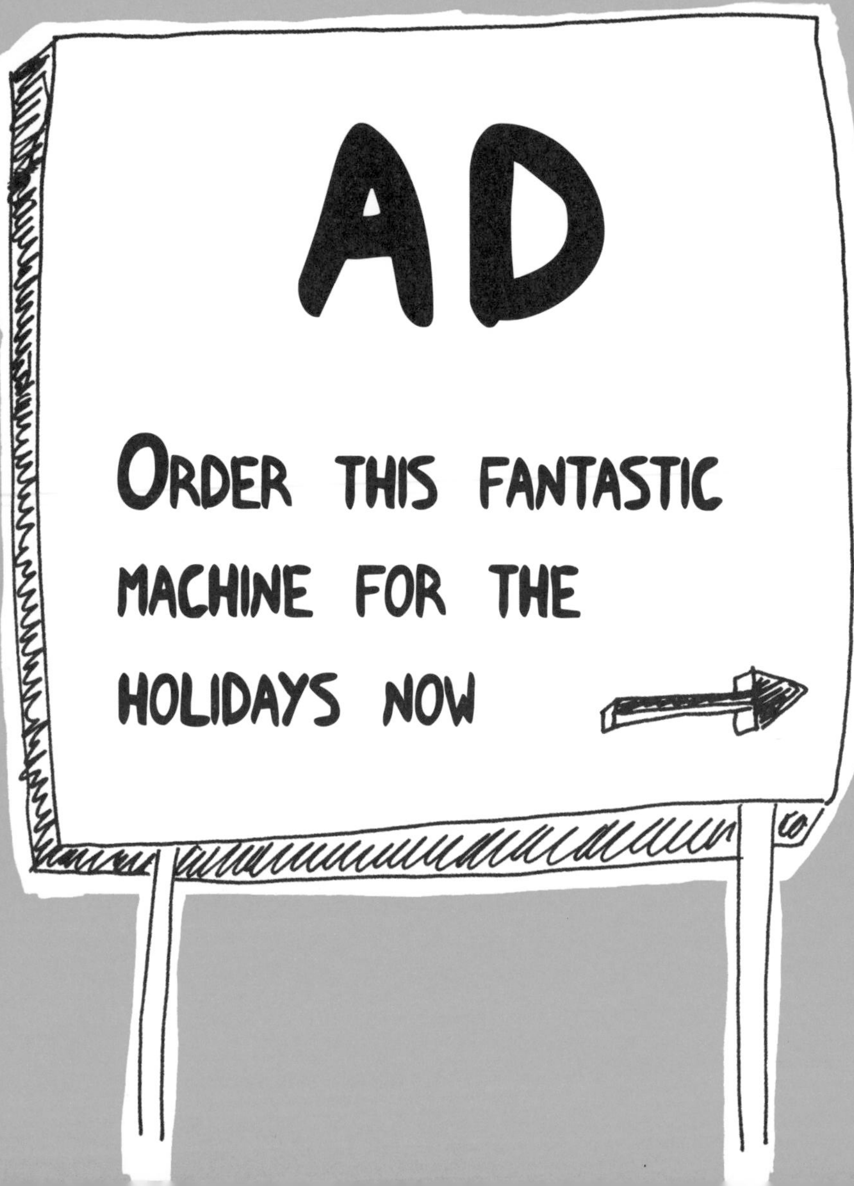
AD
ORDER THIS FANTASTIC
MACHINE FOR THE
HOLIDAYS NOW

THE MACHINE THAT CHANGES YOUR PARENTS BACK INTO KIDS SO THAT THEY UNDERSTAND YOU 200%

PARENTS CAN BE SUPER CLINGY

BUT RELAX! IT'S ONLY

BECAUSE THEY LOVE YOU

THEY TAKE YOU
EVERYWHERE WITH THEM
WHEN YOU'D RATHER
WATCH **TV**

THEY'RE
CONSTANTLY
PATTING YOU
ON THE HEAD

SUPER
GLUE

THEY HUG YOU
10 TIMES A DAY

THEY WANT TO KNOW
EVERYTHING
ABOUT YOUR LIFE

EXTRA
STRONG

THEY THINK THEY
CAN HANG OUT
IN YOUR BEDROOM

AND SOMETIMES THEY
EVEN SPY ON YOU!

TURN OVER FOR PROOF

HERE IS REALLY WHAT HAPPENED
WHEN YOU WENT TO THE BAKERY
ON YOUR OWN THE OTHER DAY

NOTE: DON'T BE MAD AT THEM, THEY'RE JUST WORRIED ABOUT YOU (BUT IF YOU'RE 42 AND THEY'RE STILL DOING IT, THEN **YOU'VE GOT A REAL PROBLEM!**)

**PARENTS
ARE OBSESSED
WITH FRUIT,
VEGETABLES,
GOING FOR WALKS,
AND LEARNING,
BUT THIS IS
A GOOD THING.
REALLY.**

*

*

JUST LOOK AT
WHAT WOULD HAPPEN
TO YOU IF THEY WEREN'T

WHAT DO YOU MAKE OF THIS?

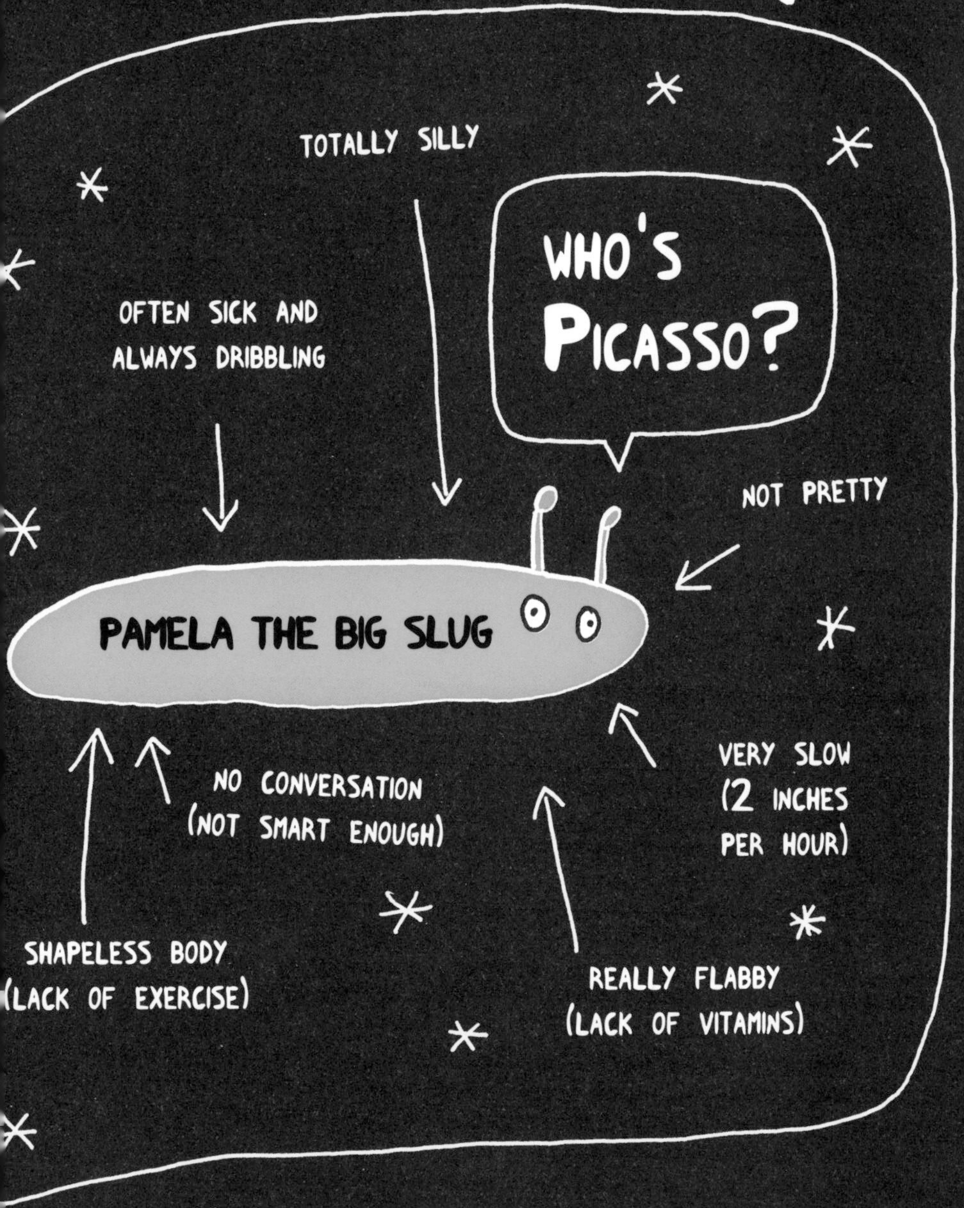

BUT AT LEAST PAMELA EATS LETTUCE!

GAME

FIND 3 MISTAKES ON THIS PAGE

ANSWERS

1: THE MOM HAS 3 LEGS
2: THE DAD HAS 3 EYES
3: PARENTS DON'T SAY **YES** TO EVERYTHING IN REAL LIFE
(FORTUNATELY, OTHERWISE THEIR CHILDREN
WOULD BE BADLY BEHAVED!)

BUT PARENTS WHO ALWAYS SAY **NO** AREN'T NORMAL EITHER

IF YOURS ARE LIKE THIS, GIVE THEM A COPY OF THIS BOOK RIGHT NOW

AND **WOW** JUST LOOK AT THE RESULTS!

BUT HERE'S **ONE OF THE WORST THINGS** ABOUT PARENTS

THEY OCCASIONALLY TELL YOU TO DO SOMETHING **WHILE THEY DO THE OPPOSITE**

THE PROOF

RUN AND BRUSH YOUR TEETH, MY DARLING

DOG BREATH

DON'T BE RUDE, ANGEL

OH #*?$! WHAT A STUPID USELESS WASTE-OF-TIME OVEN. MY BROCCOLI CASSEROLE IS BURNED! *RUDE WORD*

REMIND THEM THAT THEY SHOULD SET AN EXAMPLE!

PARENTS CAN'T STAND YOU TELLING LIES, IT MAKES THEM SICK

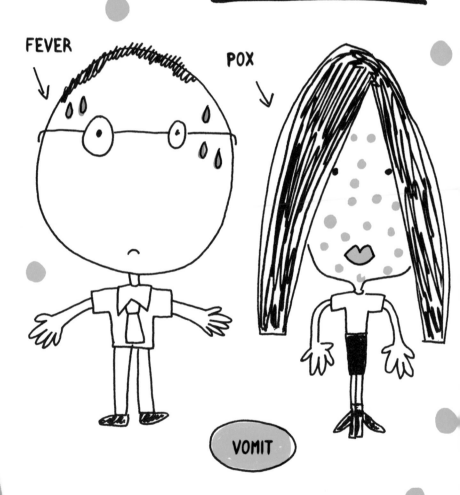

IT'S A VERY SERIOUS
ILLNESS CALLED:

SEVERE
ANTI-TRUSTITIS

WHAT'S MORE, IF YOU TELL TOO MANY LIES,
THEY WON'T GET BETTER AND WON'T BELIEVE ANTHING YOU SAY,
EVEN WHEN YOU'RE TELLING THE TRUTH **SO BE CAREFUL!**

FIRST DAY OF SCHOOL

YOUR NEW BEST FRIEND →

HAS REPEATED
THE SAME SCHOOL
YEAR 12 TIMES

GOES OUT
TO CLUBS

STOLEN
LEATHER
JACKET

YOU

AH, YES: YOUR PARENTS INSIST
ON GETTING TO KNOW
ALL YOUR FRIENDS

3 DAYS LATER

YOU, SENTENCED TO **6** MONTHS
IN PRISON FOR STEALING CANDY

IT'S <u>OBVIOUS</u> WHY:
THEY'RE AFRAID YOU'LL FALL
IN WITH THE WRONG CROWD
AND TURN OUT BADLY!

IT'S THE END OF THE YEAR

QUESTION: WHAT SHOULD YOU DO IF YOUR PARENTS PASS OUT WHEN THEY READ YOUR SCHOOL REPORT?

ALWAYS ASLEEP IN CLASS = FAILED SCHOOL

GULP

OH MY GOD!

THE ANSWERS

1. MAKE THEM SNIFF SOMETHING VERY SMELLY

2. IF THAT DOESN'T WORK, THROW A BUCKET OF COLD WATER OVER THEM

3. FINALLY AS A LAST RESORT, CALL A SPECIAL AMBULANCE

NEE NAW NEE NAWW!

SOS PARENTS

RESUSCITATION TEAM FOR BAD SCHOOL REPORTS

SOMETIMES THEY CAN'T EVEN AGREE BETWEEN THEMSELVES!

PUT YOUR **RED** PANTS ON TO GO FOR LUNCH AT GRANDMA AND GRANDPA'S

WEAR YOUR **BLUE** PANTS

REALLY ANNOYING!

HEY, GUYS, IF <u>YOU</u> <u>CAN'T</u> <u>AGREE</u>, JUST GET ME A <u>SECOND</u> <u>PAIR OF</u> <u>LEGS</u> <u>FOR MY</u> <u>BIRTHDAY</u>!

HERE ARE 2 DREAMS THAT WILL NEVER HAPPEN IN REAL LIFE

DREAM   DREAM   DREAM

DREAM

WOULD YOU LIKE
ONE OF THOSE SPECIAL
TOOTHBRUSHES
YOU ONLY HAVE
TO USE
ONCE A YEAR?

DREAM

DREA

DREAM

DREAM   DREAM

EXAMPLE 1

HA HA HA HA HA
HA HA HA HA HA
HA HA HA HA HA
HAHAHAHAHAHA
HOHOHOHOHO
HU HU HU HAHA
HIHIHIHI HAHA

LAUGHS STUPIDLY AND LOUDLY IN FRONT OF EVERYBODY

BAD HAIR DAY

GRANNY TOP

PLEATED SKIRT SOOO LAST CENTURY

YOU, DYING OF SHAME

YOUR MOM

THERE ARE TIMES SOOO EMBARRASSING

EXAMPLE 2

YOU, RED AS A BEET BECAUSE YOUR DAD HAS JUST CALLED YOU "MY SWEET WIDDLE COOCHI COO" AND **KISSED** YOU IN FRONT OF **ALL YOUR FRIENDS**

ADVICE

TELL YOUR FRIENDS THAT THEY AREN'T YOUR **REAL** PARENTS, BUT TWO CRAZY PEOPLE YOU JUST MET IN THE STREET

URGENT

Fantastic kid wishes to exchange parents immediately for parents WHO WON'T MAKE HIM DO HIS HOMEWORK AND DON'T CARE ABOUT HIS GRADES

 BUT WATCH OUT!

IT MIGHT ALL GO HORRIBLY WRONG

YOU MAY BE ACCEPTED INTO A FAMILY OF PENGUINS + MADE TO EAT RAW FISH + GET A FREEZING BEHIND BY SITTING ON ICE ALL DAY

BRRR BRRR BRRR!

YOUR NEW DAD   YOUR NEW MOM

INTO A TRIBE AT THE HEART OF THE JUNGLE

YOUR CHIEF-DAD

YOUR NEW DAD'S WIVES

DINNER FOR ALL THE FAMILY
(SNAKE AND
TARANTULA KEBABS)

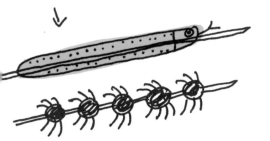

BEDROOM HUT FOR YOU AND YOUR
250 BROTHERS AND SISTERS

CONCLUSION: IT'S BETTER TO TRY
TO GET ALONG WITH YOUR PARENTS

WHATEVER YOU DO, DON'T WORRY WHEN YOUR PARENTS SEEM A BIT STRANGE (IT HAPPENS TO ALL PARENTS)

THESE ARE SOME OF THE SYMPTOMS
OF EXTREME CASES OF
"FEDUPADULTITIS"

DON'T WORRY! IT'S THE HAPPIEST ILLNESS IN THE WORLD
(AND THE AUTHOR OF THIS BOOK
HAS GOT A BAD CASE)

LA LA LA LA
HIP HIP HOORAY
CIAO, KIDS,
WE'RE OFF TO
VENICE

LA DOLCE VITA AMORE MIO ♪♪

YOUR LITTLE SUITCASE FOR YOUR WEEK WITH GRANDMA AND GRANDPA

HAVE A GREAT TIME!

YOUR PARENTS ARE ALSO PEOPLE, SO IT'S ONLY FAIR THAT THEY GET A BREAK TOO

THE GREAT MYSTERY:

YOUR PARENTS ARE NEVER IN THE SAME MOOD. THEY HAVE THEIR UPS AND DOWNS

ONE DAY THEY'RE LOVELY, BEAMING AND HAPPY

THE NEXT DAY THEY'RE REALLY AWFUL AND IN A TERRIBLE MOOD

THEY LOOK **10** YEARS OLDER!

CABBAGE HEAD

TURNIP HEAD

TO HELP YOU TO UNDERSTAND, LOOK AT THE GRAPH ON THE NEXT PAGE

- - - - >

USE THESE GRAPHS TO DECODE AND UNDERSTAND YOUR PARENTS' MOODS

YOUR DAD

HIS TEAM WINS A GAME

A GOOD, RESTFUL NIGHT'S SLEEP

EVERY MONDAY MORNING

THE HOUSE NEEDS VACUUMING

HAS A FI[GHT] WITH YOUR [...]

YOUR MOM

LANDS A GREAT CONTRACT AT WORK

FEELS THIN (CAN GET INTO HER JEANS AGAIN)

EVERY MONDAY MORNING

A BAD NIGHT WITH TERRIBLE NIGHTMARES

HAS A FIGHT WITH YOUR DA[D]

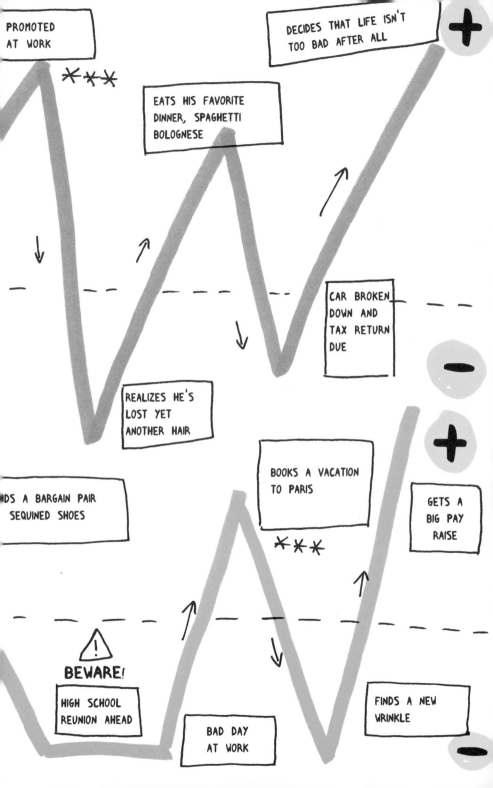

THIS IS REALLY AWFUL!

IF YOUR PARENTS **GET REALLY ANGRY** THEY CAN MAKE **DREADFUL THREATS** BECAUSE THEY DON'T KNOW WHAT TO SAY TO MAKE YOU DO AS YOU'RE TOLD

WHATEVER YOU DO, DON'T BELIEVE THEM!

RGI
(Really Good Idea)

IF YOU ABSOLUTELY DON'T WANT TO DO AS YOU'RE TOLD

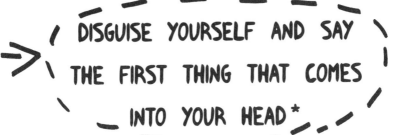

DISGUISE YOURSELF AND SAY THE FIRST THING THAT COMES INTO YOUR HEAD*

* DON'T FORGET TO USE A NEW YORK ACCENT

HI!
I'M HARRY FROM NEW YORK. YOUR SON HAS GONE OFF AROUND THE WORLD AND IS LETTING ME USE HIS ROOM. YEAAHH!

RUBBER EARS

FAKE MUSTACHE

NYC

GIANT PLASTIC HANDS AND FEET

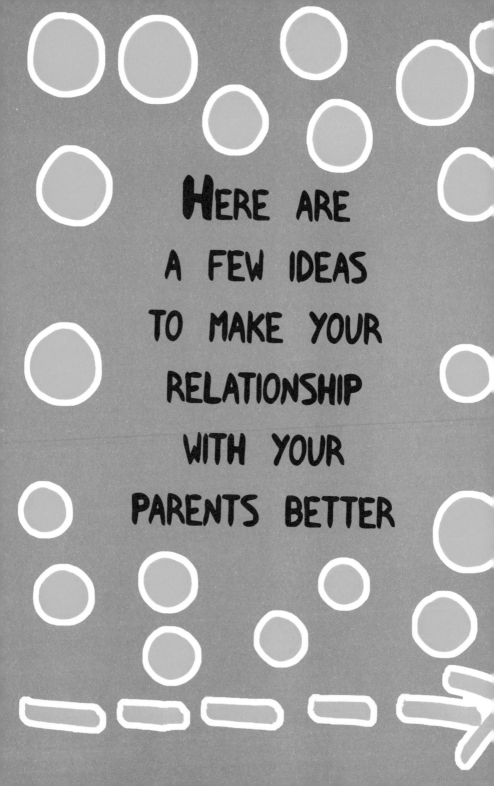

HERE ARE
A FEW IDEAS
TO MAKE YOUR
RELATIONSHIP
WITH YOUR
PARENTS BETTER

YES _(SAY THIS MORE OFTEN)_

WHAT CAN I DO TO HELP, DEAR PARENTS?

NO _(SAY THIS LESS)_

THERE'S NO WAY I'M GOING TO SET THE TABLE OR PUT MY DIRTY PLATE IN THE DISHWASHER. DREAM ON, FOOLS!

HELP YOUR PARENTS TO REALIZE THAT YOU'RE GROWING UP BY SHOWING THEM THIS PICTURE OF YOU **IN 10 YEARS TIME**

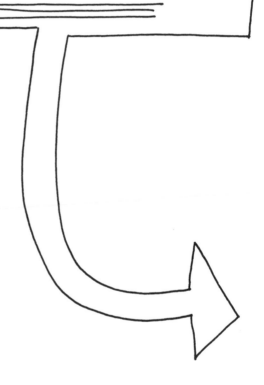

NOTE: BREAK IT TO THEM GENTLY AS THEY RISK BEING **EXTREMELY SHOCKED**

PICTURE FROM AN "AGING" APP
FOR GIRLS
OR
FOR BOYS
CHEST SIZE XL
BODY OF A CURVY MODEL
SIZE 7 FEET
VERY HAIRY
DEEP VOICE
6 FEET 6 INCHES
SIZE 14 FEET

DON'T EVEN
BOTHER TRYING

MORE THAN LIKELY
THEY'LL SAY NO

GOOD CHANCE
THEY'LL SAY YES

GO FOR IT,
SUNSHINE! IT'S
NOW OR NEVER!

WHO ARE THESE
TWO WEIRDOS?

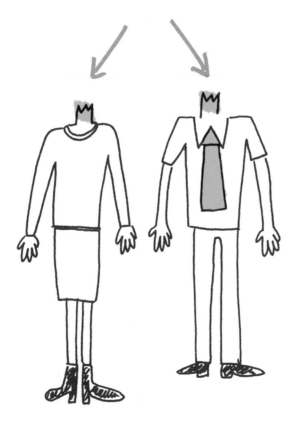

THEY'RE YOUR PARENTS
WHEN YOU'VE MADE THEM
SO MAD THEIR HEADS
EXPLODED, SO DON'T MAKE
THEM MAD AND EVERYTHING
WILL RUN SMOOTHLY

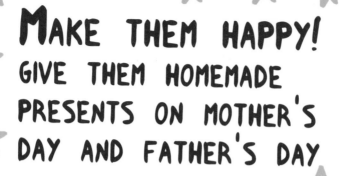

MAKE THEM HAPPY!
GIVE THEM HOMEMADE PRESENTS ON MOTHER'S DAY AND FATHER'S DAY

FATHER'S DAY

↑
UNDERPANTS MADE
FROM PASTA BOWS

↑
MACARONI TIE

↑
MINI BOW TIE MADE
FROM PASTA

MOTHER'S DAY

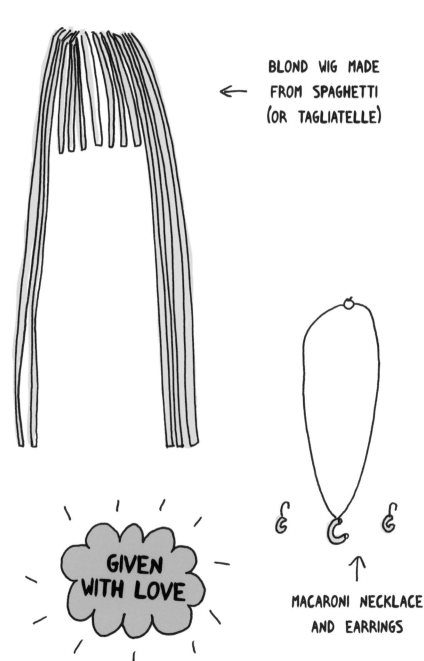

BLOND WIG MADE
FROM SPAGHETTI
(OR TAGLIATELLE)

GIVEN
WITH LOVE

MACARONI NECKLACE
AND EARRINGS

IT'S GOO[D]

SOME RANDOM ADVICE

- TALK ABOUT EVERYTHING WITH YOUR PARENTS
- ASK THEM QUESTIONS
- SAY WHAT YOU THINK AND HOW YOU'RE FEELING
- TELL THEM ABOUT YOUR DAY

I HATE CAULIFLOWER

WHAT DO YOU THINK ABOUT NUCLEAR POWER?

WHY DO YOU SAY THAT?

TO TALK!

TALKING WILL HELP YOU UNDERSTAND EACH OTHER BETTER

AND YIPPEE!
EVERYTHING'S FINE!

TAKE TIME TO LAUGH WITH YOUR PARENTS EVERY DAY

EVEN IF YOUR DAD IS AN ACCOUNTANT IN A GIANT GRAVEYARD

AND YOUR MOM SELLS
CHOCOLATE SKULLS

HOW MANY WOULD
YOU LIKE?

HOORAY FOR HALLOWEEN!

IF THEY HAVEN'T GOT A SENSE OF HUMOR,
TICKLE THEM UNDER THE ARMS
WITH THIS FEATHER

HA HA HA
HA HA HA

BLANK PAGE: STICK A PHOTO OF YOUR PARENTS HERE

OR DRAW THEM

SMILE!

DEAREST READER, YOU REALLY DIDN'T NEED TO READ THIS WHOLE BOOK (YOU'D HAVE BEEN BETTER OFF GOING TO THE SWIMMING POOL OR MOVIES) BECAUSE PARENTS ARE THERE FOR ONE REASON ONLY: **TO LOVE THEIR CHILDREN** AND ALL THE REST REALLY DOESN'T MATTER TOO MUCH!

BUT THANKS FOR READING IT ANYWAY, I'M REALLY THRILLED!

THE AUTHOR DISGUISED AS A MUSHROOM SO NOBODY WILL RECOGNIZE HER WHEN SHE GOES WALKING IN THE WOODS

IS THIS REALLY THE END?
WELL, NO, BECAUSE THE RELATIONSHIP
BETWEEN PARENTS AND CHILDREN
IS NEVER ENDING, LIKE:

THE SKY

THE SEA

LAUGHTER

IMAGINATION

POETRY

LOVE

SO, SEE YOU SOON!

SIGNED: FRANÇOIZE

Published in the U.S.A. in March 2014 by Walker Books for
Young Readers, an imprint of Bloomsbury Publishing, Inc.
www.bloomsbury.com

Bloomsbury books may be purchased for business or
promotional use. For information on bulk purchases please
contact Macmillan Corporate and Premium Sales Department at
specialmarkets@macmillan.com

Library of Congress Cataloging-in-Publication Data
available upon request • ISBN 978-0-8027-3744-1

Publisher, Nathan: Jean-Christophe Fournier
Art Director: Lieve Louwagie • Design: Albane Rouget
Proofreader: Christiane Keukens-Poirier
Production: Lucile Davesnes-Germaine and Bénédicte Gaudin
Photogravure: Axiome

Printed in China by Toppan Excel, Guangshou City, Guangdong
10 9 8 7 6 5 4 3 2 1

PLEASE GIVE A COPY OF THIS
BOOK TO ALL YOUR FRIENDS
SO THEY FINALLY
GET TO UNDERSTAND
THEIR PARENTS!